D1416512

Know Your Emotions

SCARED IS...

by Cheyenne Nichols

CAPSTONE PRESS
a capstone imprint

My heart is pounding loudly.

I jump and gasp and stare.

My words won't seem to come out right—

you *bet* that I am scared!

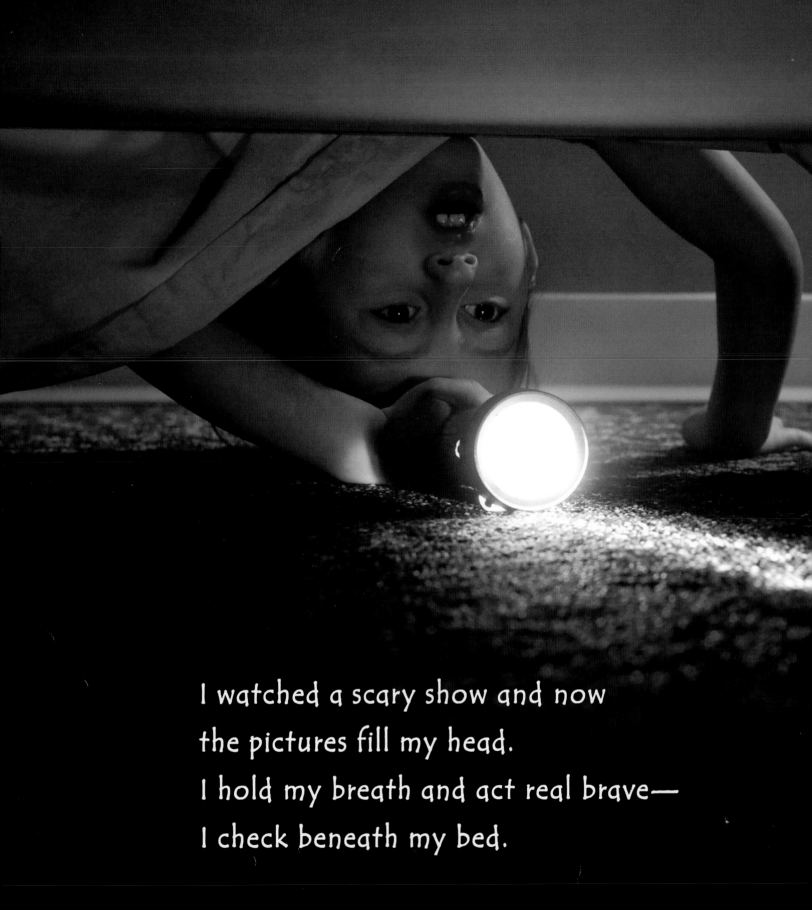

I watched a scary show and now
the pictures fill my head.
I hold my breath and act real brave—
I check beneath my bed.

His owner says he wants to play,
but I wish I could hide.
I start to sweat. My feet go cold
because I'm terrified!

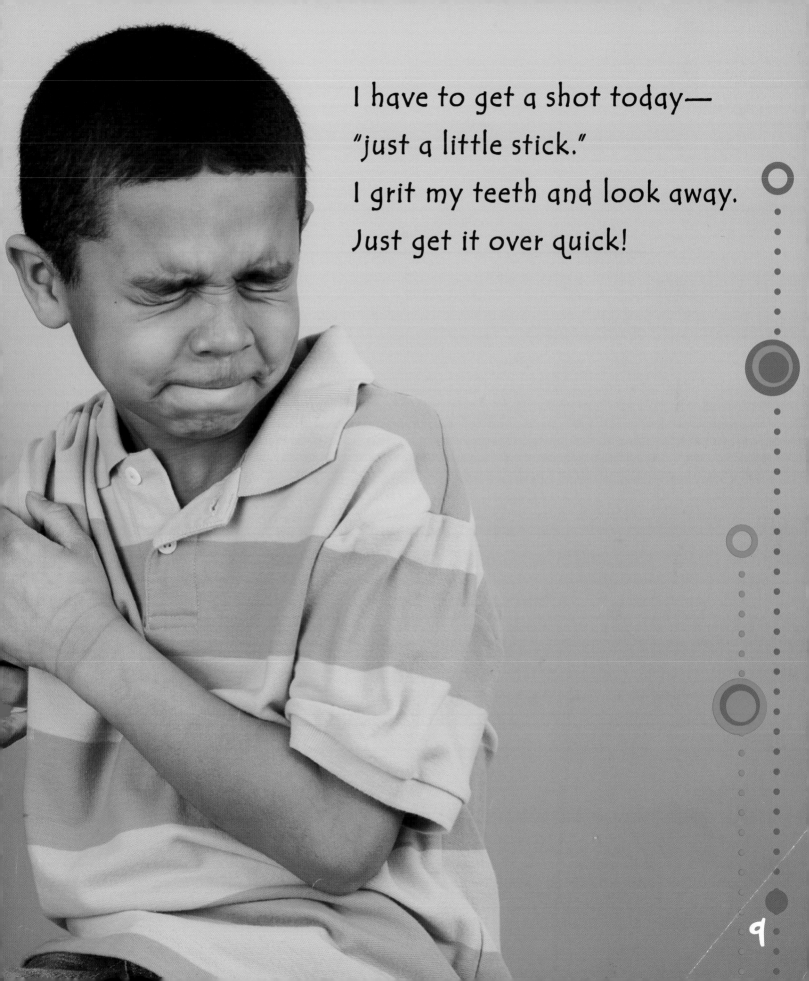

I have to get a shot today—
"just a little stick."
I grit my teeth and look away.
Just get it over quick!

I trudge up front. The class awaits.
My pulse pounds in my ears.
Doing problems on the board
is one of my big fears.

I'm strapped in, scared, and buckled tight.
I'm whipping round and round.
I'm safe! I'm fine! I tell myself,
and soon I'm back on ground.

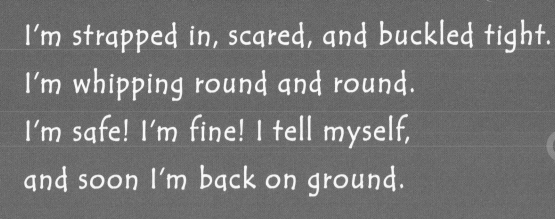

13

My knees begin to bend and shake.

That water seems so deep.

My feet are frozen to the ground.

I'm scared to make the leap!

15

I turn around—my stomach drops.
The rows stretch out for miles.
It's like a spinning, scary ride—
my mom's lost in the aisles.

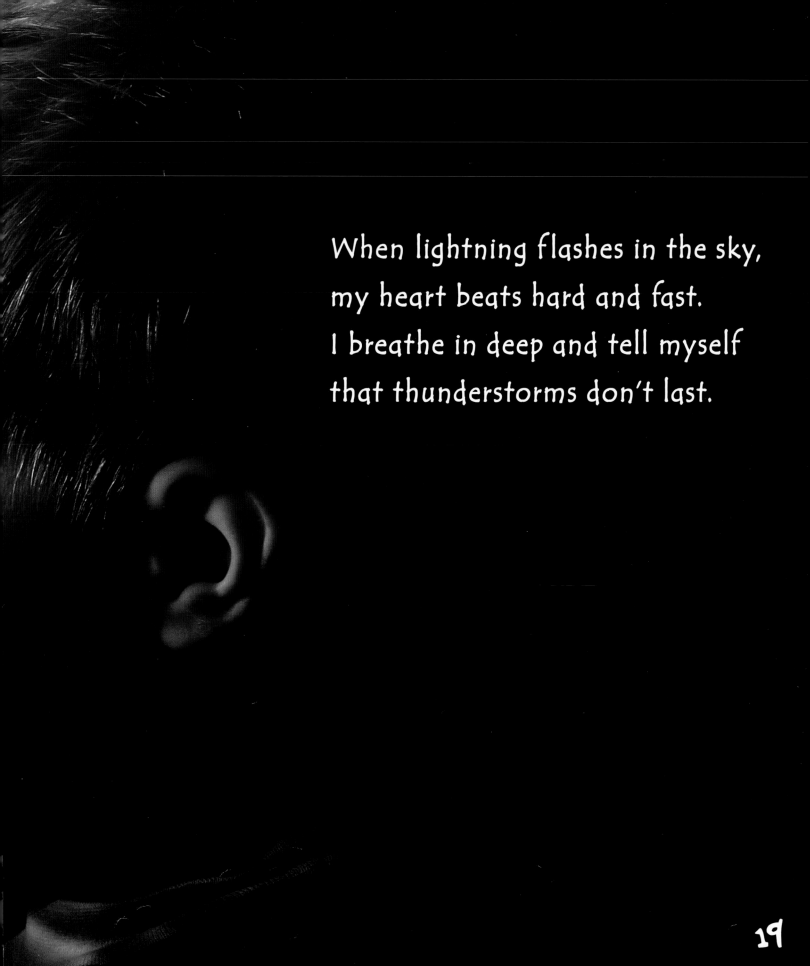

When lightning flashes in the sky,
my heart beats hard and fast.
I breathe in deep and tell myself
that thunderstorms don't last.

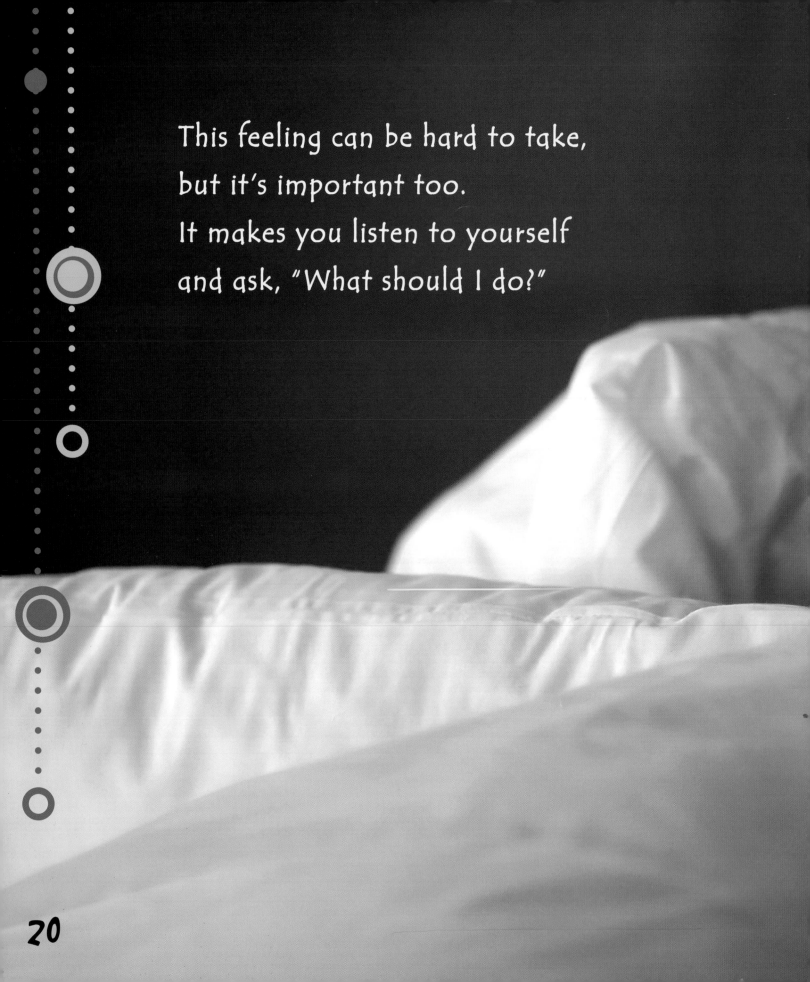

This feeling can be hard to take,
but it's important too.
It makes you listen to yourself
and ask, "What should I do?"

Glossary

gasp—to quickly breathe in because you are surprised or scared

pulse—the steady beat of your heart moving blood through your body

terrify—to frighten greatly

trudge—to walk slowly and with effort

whip—to move or pull something quickly

Read More

Aboff, Marcie. *Everyone Feels Scared Sometimes.* Everyone Has Feelings. Minneapolis: Picture Window Books, 2010.

Annunziata, Jane, and Marc Nemiroff. *Sometimes I'm Scared.* Washington, D.C.: Magination Press, 2009.

Bingham, Jane. *Everybody Feels Scared.* Everybody Feels. New York: Crabtree Pub., 2008.

INTERNET SITES

FactHound offers a safe, fun way to find Internet sites related to this book. All of the sites on FactHound have been researched by our staff.

Here's all you do:

Visit www.facthound.com

Type in this code: 9781429660457

 Check out projects, games and lots more at
www.capstonekids.com

INDEX

A+ Books are published by Capstone Press,
151 Good Counsel Drive, P.O. Box 669, Mankato, Minnesota 56002.
www.capstonepub.com

Books published by Capstone Press are manufactured with paper
containing at least 10 percent post-consumer waste.

Library of Congress Cataloging-in-Publication Data
Nichols, Cheyenne.
  Scared is... / by Cheyenne Nichols.
     p. cm.—(A+ books. Know your emotions)
  Summary: "Photographs and short rhyming verses describe how it feels to be scared"— Provided by
publisher.
  Includes bibliographical references and index.
  ISBN 978-1-4296-6045-7 (library binding) ISBN 978-1-4296-7053-1 (paperback)
  1. Fear in children—Juvenile literature. 2. Fear—Juvenile literature. 3. Emotions in children—Juvenile
literature. I. Title. II. Series.
  BF723.F4S25 2012
  152.4'6—dc22   2011006125

Credits

Jeni Wittrock, editor; Alison Thiele, designer; Svetlana Zhurkin, media researcher; Sarah Schuette, photo stylist;
    Marcy Morin, scheduler; Eric Manske, production specialist

Photo Credits

Alamy/Ace Stock Limited, 12–13
Capstone Studio/Karon Dubke, cover, 4–5, 6–7, 8–9, 14–15, 16–17
iStockphoto/Rob Friedman, 20–21; Slobodan Vasic, 18–19
Shutterstock/AJP, 1; Etienne du Preez, 18 (lightning); Hasan Shaheed, 10–11; Zurijeta, 2–3

Note to Parents, Teachers, and Librarians

This Know Your Emotions book uses full color photographs and a nonfiction format to introduce the concept of being
scared. *Scared Is...* is designed to be read aloud to a pre-reader or to be read independently by an early reader.
Photographs help listeners and early readers understand the text and concepts discussed. The book encourages further
learning by including the following sections: Glossary, Read More, Internet Sites, Index. Early readers may need assistance
using these features.

Printed in the United States of America in North Mankato, Minnesota.

032011   006110CGF11